50 Poems About None-Such Nonsense

CARMAN TIMARA BENOIT

CARMAN BENOIT

Copyright © 2012 Carman Benoit

All rights reserved.

ISBN: 978-0-9953094-0-1
ISBN-13: 978-0995309401

DEDICATION

This book is dedicated to Robert Christopher Johnson (May 25, 1986 - Oct 11, 2015). Celebrating your adventurous spirit, your powerful mind, your drop dead gorgeousness, your desire for peace and equity, and even your crazy. The shame in your mental illness, was others fear of stigma and desire to hide you away to avoid embarrassment. Well "sweetness", I loved you like no other, and promise to graffiti your name on every wall I see.

- CTB

CARMAN BENOIT

50 Poems About None-Such Nonsense

CONTENTS

A lot of fucking poetry!

Pick a page.

It's all nonsense.
I have the runcible spoon to prove.
Not a marriage.
But the owl and the pussycat,
On a journey to find the ring.
My tiger, the kitty on a pea green boat,
an old lady in glasses the owl.
Next the ring to be found.
Rather not from the bull,
But to the bull.
A right of passage,
The owl to witness.

Destiny subdued by the pebbles of glory.
Defeat never a possibility.
Jonesing for a breath of the life you once had.
Reality check on the waves that distort it.
Sobering cries from the drunks that had drowned you,
In memorabilia of Elvis Presley.
Lips curling around the bathtub rim.
In order to deep throat surrealism and abstract themselves.
Travelling for real in the rainforests of TV.
So give me a slice of that pie!

The sagest whispers spoke,
Heard from the kingdom of St. Louis.
I refute you not dear lady belle,
I'll simply huff "AHHH PHOOEY!".

What if I gave to you,
A bathtub built for two?
How happy would you be,
To splash along with me?
We could be the crew,
of a yacht upon the blue.
And we' never cry boohoo
On the S.S. Pink Bubbles.
We could grab a cup of tea,
And sail upon the sea.
Where would we go to?
Down through some bayou?
Gliding oh so free,
Way too full of glee,
On the S.S. Pink Bubbles.

For the love of synergy,
The only calm I find.
Electric compliments,
Trigger synaptic jubilation.
Amplified shivers wash-over,
Like bobbing buoyant tickles on my skin.

May everything be wove in wool,
And n'er she be a wolven stole.
N'er pancakes or cake pans,
N'er trampolined handstands.
Or, liquored up snickers,
About somebody's nickers.
For, yesteryears mainstay,
Is today's jaunt on the main causeway.

Waxing poetic,
At the likes of a camel,
Will only get spit in your eye.
Your time is best served,
Talking about love,
With the ever clinging fungi.
With your butt on a log,
And your toes in the moss,
Cawing a song at the crows.
With your hair in a knot,
And your brain on a loom,
Weaving words that nobody knows.

When I rumble in my walk.
And if stumble in my talk.
You must swallow a slow on my pause.
My non lateral conversation you'll hear cause.
No tires on bones and beans and bums
But if the non vetted will here the tourist comes.
And, have you of charge.
Ice creams and China art on the large.
A tired that swing of family can be
It really was only as what it could be.

Tipping the boundaries to see the ambien zoo.
Having signs in sequence',
Ah long a linger blue.
Dinbanging the spouts of autocorrect. Nothing to chime in frain,
Loss Daddy's spectacles.
AfibDibday.

Let me tell you about this girl,
Who spent her life portraying a world.
She was her world.
She made her world a spitting image of what she had seen.
She had seen it all.
But her world was poor and unnourished.
So she sat for many weeks and pondered a solution.
As so, she was getting slimmer by the moment.
And, her world crops had decreased in abundance.
Then she came up with a realization,
Her world could supply food for her population.
So she cut off her arm,
As she screamed "Earthquake in China!"
Then her other leg went.
And, there went Russia.
Then her arms went.
And, there went North America.
Total destruction of a world.
The world that was hers.
The world that she was.

I have lots of figments.
They grow outside upon my figment tree.
Once based in a foundation of truth,
They are no longer allowed to be realized,
So now they run amok in my imagination.

Nutty opossum,
Wet and stank.
Wobble, Fobble, Bobble
Bobble, Bobble, Bobble.

"Be quiet" I snear at the,
Happy chewing audience.
"If fat deposits in sling shots,
It's what have driven you here?"
Save your pennies for napkin,
So when you weep in pain,
They'll clear away hearts distress,
And every burning wayward tear.
The girl won't shake or shimmer,
From this day forth upon stage so slick.
She took her run with her dads shotgun,
And sped off on a grizzly bear.

This dirty dog is my church,
Where I perform my deeds.
Good and true the acts,
With only few that sees.
In cahoots with the bar maid,
She knows which strings to pull.
To ignite my charity,
For those lacking of the dole.
Confessing all my sins,
Taking my sweet time,
I turn my head behind me,
At the pending line.
I apologize profusely,
For my dallying delay,
Safe travels does she grants me,
And sends me on my way.

In a breath, the cold breeze sent shiver down my back, making real and surreal the experience of the holidays. It felt as if it was a rare moment when a bubble floats along the surface of still water for no reason. Just gliding on surface tension waiting for the inevitable bursting poof.

I come in haste to see the light,
Before it fades away.
A tribute of some tea and cheese,
To feed us for the day.
With willow wisps and a piece of chalk,
We redesign the town.
Some thrift store sheets, a rope and clips,
We make a fancy gown.
Kick off our shoes and jiffy our toes,
Dancing wildly down the street.
We curtsy, smile, and say "adieu",
To everyone we meet.

Asido, Asido,
It's hard as hell.
Staying calm,
When I want to yell.
Asido, Asido,
Using my ear,
Hearing words,
I don't want to hear.
Asido, Asido,
Is the way,
I do As-I-do

As well as I say.
If I lied upon a whack-a-mole,
I could live a happy life.
Cheap tricks and a back massage,
Could do this mighty nice.
When lunch rolls round,
And I grab all my ticket stubs,
Cash em at the concession,
For a soda and some subs.
I'll knock the kids off my machine,
The round 2 of my snooze.
Man of man this could only be better
With some popcorn and some booze.

I wonder if experimented,
With "Just for Men",
Would lochs of red and brown,
Have more bravado?
Saying "Fiery, Feisty, Fist to Cuffs"
Has anyone ever asked,
A tailor skilled with threads?
Fitted shirts with French cuffs,
Oh and dress me to the centre?
In a way that NO TOE will SHOW!
In my pool the sharks swim,
On the shallow side taking easy pray,
I looking to swagger in behind them,
And dashingly make my own means,
Sauntering and sloshing, just swimmingly!

It's hard as hell.
Staying calm,
When I want to yell.
Asido, Asido,
Using my ear,
Hearing words,
I don't want to hear.
Asido, Asido,
Is the way,
I do As-I-do,
As well as I say.

Sleep deprived,
The music of the theremin,
Strokes the nodes,
Of my reptilian brain,
Like eerie alien lullabies.
The unpretentious chairs,
Old, sturdy,
Have asserted,
That quality need not be replaced.
Coffee jittered,
Leg sways in shake,
Vaguely seductive?
Ardently thoughtful?
Or maybe that Parkinson's shake,
That trembles through a sieve,
Of genetic uncertainty.
Zippers zipping,
A prevalent jar.
As each individual,
Checks an rechecks,

(cont.)
If there junk is as neat as can be.
Sadly it's not.
Books and papers and wallet and keys,
Jostle and shimmy loose
the fine inner order of the bags.
Little hill with hazy cloud,
Makes me yearn for the sun dogs,
I just kissed goodbye.
And the cowboy,
I'll kiss hello.
I challenge the chefs,
That glue that cellulose plastic on top.
Was there ever really a chef?
Or a patented trademark,
Rusery to the willfully blind business exec.
Who in this moment,
Is just to tired to question,
Let alone argue the merits of it's skill.
Retractable, telescopic,
With wheels and stairs,
Retractable, telescopic,
With wheels and stairs,
When sudden realization,
Of a mistaken identity,
Causes giggles,
And brings more sense to the world.

J'aime jaune au jour d'hui.
Jolie jaune Jolie jaune Jolie.

What beauty lay between the broken,
Shattered glass shimmers so much brighter.
A mosaic of treasure in a pack rats nest,
N'er to beheld unless it's wholly intact in it's unrifledness.
A twisted shimmy of pride and humility,
Aloof and brazen clash,
Like waves crashing on the sifted sand.
Blown bubbles glazed bursting,
Before secret notes are cast off in bottles,
Adrift on the oceans skin.

I'm not very tired,
I'm not tired at all.
My golden ambition,
To stare at the wall.
To twiddle my fingers,
And fidget my toes,
To stretch out my legs,
And crinkle my nose.
Adjust myself,
From left to right,
I'll try it again,
I'll try all the night.
I'll grab a short novel,
To boring to read,
I read the first page,
Then slow down the speed.
My outer appendages,
I'll try to warm up.
Some tea for my nerves,
Pip! Pip!, just one cup.
I'll pile pillows,

(cont.)
On top of my head,
Try to lay flatly,
Pretend I am dead.
 But the sweet chirpy sound,
Of the birds as they cries,
Evokes sleepy time curse,
On top of my eyes.
The sunbeams peak through,
And burn at my skull,
Till the sum of mathematics,
Is nothing but null.
The dream caster sneaks in,
Selecting his crew,
Of dreamy time people,
And sequence to view.
My shoulders relax,
My mouth all agape,
Embracing the set
Enjoying the tape

I tiptoe tall proud luminescent,
Feeling like a glowing light,
Choreographs the float of hand,
Surrounds me reflection of white.
Sitting cross legged feeling the dirt,
Surging love feelings bring out a smile.
My blood tingles warm in all of my body.
Harness that energy then walk a mile.

My hypnotic foot,
Is concerned about,
They pyramid of stability,
And jellyfish on the beach.
My hypnotic hand,
Fears nothing.
Just striving for speed,
And no regard for literary rule.
My hypnotic eyes,
A gopher of such.
From thought to word,
And, to "Eureka!".
My hypnotic brain,
Wants tempo,
While reconstructing,
Language use.

Sometimes the sleepy poet,
Let's predictive text have its win.
A silly challenge, a Hoosiers toast,
Slurred spoken to have hurly spin.
The socks don't bake by themselves,
They need custard to survive.
Filled leggy jelly toasted toe jam,
Flavours to keep alive.
Monster truck slides In muck,
And rapidly down hills,
A basket team will surely scream.
Yahoos all a shrill.

I'll keep quiet on the megaphone,
And, keep still on the Merry-go-round.
Just to shape me wisely,
And, know how to be let down
Your bottles rest in my hands,
Not a single one left for you.
I travel to the best ones,
When I'm feeling blue.

A pig and a poet,
My grace is crass.
A delicate fleur,
With a porno ass.
Quiet, demure,
A violent tongue,
A ladybug,
Hornet stung.
Another fucking sunset,
Pubic lice,
Whimsical heartbeats,
Gamblers dice.
Made up words,
Shakespearian theft,
Devonshire cream.
A palet cleft.
A murder of crows,
Crows that kill,
A romantic fuck,
To fill the bill.

Scraping off the rust on,
The underbelly of the bin.
I walk it down the path,
Funnacity permitted,
And practice my log driving waltz.

There's no where to go,
My pencil full of lead,
Making up reasons,
That I shouldn't be dead.
Guts inside my throat,
Spinning topsy-turvy,
Questioning my trails,
"Should I be so nervy?"
Think of Taj Mahal,
On the head of a pin,
Amplifying dreams,
To an unbearable din.
Occupying life,
Building castles in the sky,
Staying in my skin,
It's the only reason why!

I wish authored limericks,
That still haunt my mind.
In the grungy bathrooms.
When I was caught in a bind.
That lass from Dundy had great fame,
Not one of her stories a bore.
The antics that she mused in,
brought laughter on every stall door.

I did, didn't I?
Didn't I did?
Walk the tow backwards,
With a kid named Syd?
Didn't he do that?
Or didn't he did?
Paint on the walls,
With a purple squid?
I think I even saw you?
Oh doodley you do?
Somethings are so muddled,
On the big city avenue?

It is the first time calm set in,
A subtle breeze,
With sand and dust,
Flitting across the landscape,
On a foreign moon.
Orchestra and bass,
Tune and rumble,
Drowning out the ear buzzes,
And distracting from the cracks and aches.
Distant traffic,
A dull polish,
Defines,
Predicts,
The swaddled calm,
That will forever influence our lives.

Tiptoeing tipsy in the tulips,
To reno the lilac bush.
A clearer path I will make,
As I clip and twist and push.
There no room for grown ups coming.
It's the secret path of child.
A little place to save their face,
when they go completely wild.
I swirl and scratch and weave and twist.
To make a lovely arch,
With a hop and a duck, and a leap, and a salute,
To where the kids will surely march.

Floating tip toe.
Toe floating thought.
I start to feel smart again,
And my big toes says I'm not.
I say "I'll step on you real hard,
If your gonna speak your mind".
The wiggles and whispers they had,
Would surely be bind
For Royal domain the indeed,
Upon my dirty laces.
A twist right here, and a twirl over there
Could land me on my faces.

You screech the chalk across the board.
And ask, "Why don't you understand that 2+2 makes 4?"
"I'm sorry, I don't disagree, but must you be so mean?"
I sing, "I just prefer the $\sqrt{16}$."
It's aiming for the stars and getting the moon,
or when i'm broke I like -2x-2.

I have fort,
Beneath the fig,
And aluminum umbrella dryer.
Sheltered life,
It's cool and damp,
With wet clothing on the wire.
Wall of rose,
All thick and thorn,
Tells the humans to beware.
Spider webs,
With bugs and slugs,
Only the cats come in with care.
I have tea,
Two chairs and slab,
In my secret hiding place.
Time alone,
To cure my ills,
Till I feel I'll show my face.

It's a great day to toast,
And dance bout like a fool,
To slosh, and to wade,
In my crazy gene pool.
I'll concuss all my marbles,
In a clickity-click-clack-bobble.
Majorette of the parade,
Doing a gin-sipping teetotal.
Slip down to the graveyard,
And pull the corpses from their plots,
Then waltz in frenzied swirls,
Till their qualified cosmonauts.
Blow puffs of smokes at garden gnomes,
Crunching down some more cures.
It's the natural law inanity,
That life don't come with brochures.
So sometimes when mediocre,
That is your running best.
And when you're besting out those running times,
It's just because your blessed.
It's too late when you've been showing off,
To truly admit defeat.
Something will come, I'm smart, I'm great,
At thinking on my feet.
Don't say "Think on you feet"
When your mind isn't quite there.
Because feet are irrelevant,
When you can float in the air.
There is a flip side to this,
When there's no stumps on your trunks,
Is that when floating up fails,
You'll feel painful Ka-thunks.

I'm profoundly aware of my madness.
The rigid crack,
That runs deeper than the Mariana Trench.
It swallowed the sea.
Now we are unable to swim the channel.
As the starfishes dry up,
And all the adults silently stare in horror,
While the little mink's peeps,
Bounce confusingly off the bare faced walls.
Laying curse upon our souls.

Clamming up,
Is cast with consequence.
Clamming up,
Compounds combusting compunction.
Clamming up,
Castrates and quells commotion.
Clamming up,
Credits paper collared criminals,
Clamming up,
Who confiscate contributions.
Clamming up,
For my creamy community convocation.
Clamming up,
Calmly claiming cut-rate commissions,
Questioning my quilly comeuppance.
Clamming up
Is a calamity.

An old man dies.
Open his books.
And an arrow flies.
Sidelong looks,
Of scornful eyes,
Screaming "You crooks!!!"
Festering wounds covered and scarred,
Till is his death were left unmarred.

Ivory towers,
Built of sacrifice,
Sin and silence,
Entitle the owners,
To echo righteously,
Down below;
"If you only knew,
If you only knew,
If you only knew,
How my ancestors and I,
Suffered on our knees,
Feigning sweetness,
In the bitter saltiness,
Then you'd know…
What you should know,
That your plight isn't bad,
That fight won't be had,
Because your suffering,
Is of your own making,
That you just don't know how,
To suck it up."

Fine fuckery,
And foot quackery,
Smashdashery,
Filigree,
Spellbindery,
Phraseology,
Done so perfectly!

A fine lacquer box
With a broken case-tete.
A copper tube shower
To get me all wet.
A suddenly scribble
On the paint of a door
A singular stone,
Drilled for its core.

Craving the zest of an orange.
We cannot score the rind,
If the suspended mesh bag,
Is not left behind.
Perfect, levitated humans,
We definitely are not.
But leaving fruit on the counter,
Will surely lead to rot.
I just want a scratch, and a sniff,
That is only skin deep.
But the lashes and the gashes,
Leaves us crying in a heap.

If you push the envelope,
I will not catch it.
It will slide up on air.
Cascade down without a flit.
I will stare in your eye deep,
Watching the retina flecks.
Unobservant of your message,
And what's coming next.
Taste the sour on your breath,
Taking in what I will,
Down it with some tequila,
And then chase it with a pill.
Chanting out my surly dismay,
Bouncing on my foot balls.
Locking up my haunches,
To taking the comings falls.
And the snot starts running,
Bubbling out like a rabid dog,
Eyes wild and alive,
For the monologue.
That idles of dare,
Or, menace of fringe.
Will only result,
In a crackling singe.

Shuffle the feet upon the mat,
I tip to you to show my hat.
Is storm out proud, that's what I do,
All to shout a new "coo coo".

Ok...what now?
Midget wrestling?
Waxing poetic,
About blowing your O-ring?
Shall we share a plate of crabs?
So we can both itch,
And itch, and itch,
And scowl and bitch?
Poet-ing for calm?
Is ludicrously bad,
Just suck it up princess,
And do you prose MAD!!!!

I forgot the rules,
of mousehood.
Be quiet where,
You stood.
Don't stand out.
Don't leave a trail,
Don't reach for greed,
Or you'll lose your tail.
Suffer hunger,
And only then,
Race for glory.
With all you can.

ABOUT THE AUTHOR

Don't be fooled by this section. I'm supposed to tell you about myself in third person. I'm supposed to tell you about where I came from, my trials and tribulations, and my grand accomplishments. I will say I had a great many accomplishments to my name. But, for the most part I am an exemplary specimen of human failure. But really, anything that makes me interesting, is really none of your fucking business. All the best.

www.ingramcontent.com/pod-product-compliance
Lightning Source LLC
Chambersburg PA
CBHW070757050426
42452CB00010B/1875